In book 2 "Ghost Monkey," Kate and Marvin enter Monkey Hollow looking for Danger. Instead of finding the black dog, they discover a monkey with a white face inside a tree house. Also, from the tree house Kate and Marvin notice strange-looking cats roaming around Mrs. Nichols' yard.

Kate and Marvin know that the weird cats are after them.

A NEW Science Fiction Chapter Book
For Second, Third, and Fourth Grade Readers

Alien Cat

Written by Sharon Oberne
Illustrated by Bob Reese

©Alien Bleepers, 2009
Aro Publishing LLC

ISBN 978-0-89868-617-3 hard bound
ISBN 978-0-89868-618-0 soft bound

Contents

Chapter One: Run!

Kate ran until her lungs started to hurt. She had to stop and catch her breath.

"We have to keep moving," said Marvin.

Kate glared at him.

Marvin stood there with his hands on his hips staring back at Kate. Then, he muttered something and rolled his eyes. Kate stuck out her tongue. She nearly bit it, when she heard a twig snap.

Marvin said, "Let's go!"

Well, he did not bother to wait for Kate. Marvin took off.

Kate could not believe Marvin had left her behind!

Kate stumbled after him.

One moment Kate saw Marvin running ahead of her and then he vanished.

Kate ran faster trying to find him. Where was he? Branches were sticking out everywhere. Kate had to be careful not to get poked in the eye.

Oops! Kate stumbled. She fell on top of something. It was Marvin!

"Ouch! Get off me!" he yelled.

Quickly, Kate rolled off.

Marvin got up. "Take my hand."

Kate grabbed it. Marvin pulled her up. "I shouldn't have left you behind like that."

Marvin and Kate ran through the woods together.

"Are we going the right way?" asked Kate.

"I don't know," Marvin mumbled. "Let's just keep going."

They ran until the grass started to move.

Chapter Two: The Trap

It was all around them. Kate and Marvin were lifted off the ground.

They were trapped inside a green net.

The netting was rough against Kate's skin. She peered through the holes looking at the ground. Marvin moved and elbowed her in the ribs.

"Stop it!" mumbled Kate.

"Something bit me," Marvin whined. "I think it was a mosquito."

Well, there was more than one mosquito. A large one with long legs landed on Kate's hand. She slapped the insect with her other hand and it smeared on her. Kate wiped her hand.

"Cut it out!" Marvin cried. "That's disgusting."

"Oops," Kate remarked. "I didn't realize
these were your pants."

Marvin did not say a word. He dug his heel
in the netting trying to get away from Kate.

"We can't just hang here. We need to find a
way out," mumbled Marvin.

"If we had a pair of scissors, we could cut
through the netting," said Kate.

"Yeah...*knuckle brain*, but we don't!"

Kate turned her head towards him and
hissed, "Don't call me, *knuckle brain*!"

Marvin pinched her!

"Ouch!" grumbled Kate.

Marvin laughed.

Kate did not like being teased. She was about to say something when Marvin covered her mouth with his hand.

"Sh-h…something's coming."

Chapter Three: Dragonfly Bleep

It strolled in the clearing under them. A gray, furry creature with long, pointed ears was scanning the area. Kate and Marvin hoped it would leave. Then for no apparent reason, it stopped and started walking backwards.

'What in the world?' thought Kate.

The alien cat was wearing a pink-jeweled collar and a bleep, resembling a dragonfly.

It lifted its paw and began pressing buttons on the dragonfly bleep.

A screen appeared in the air coming from the

dragonfly's stomach. The letters 'D, I, K, and U,' flashed on the screen.

"Do I Know You?" muttered Kate.

"No, you don't!" answered Marvin.

Next, on the screen appeared the letters, F, W, I, and W,' along with the words, looking for black dog, followed by the letters, I, O, and H.

Kate stared at the screen. She was not sure what the letters said.

But, Marvin knew. "For What It's Worth…looking for black dog…I'm Out of Here."

The screen vanished. The alien cat started to walk away, until Marvin whispered Danger's name.

The alien cat looked up at them. It used its paw again to activate the dragonfly bleep.

However, this time the jewels on the dragonfly lit up like lights on a Christmas tree.

The alien cat's voice was heard coming from the bleep. "You speak English...*good*!"

Its eyes glowed as it continued, "*Danger*, what an interesting name for the black dog! Where is the thief?"

"Thief!" Kate growled. "He's no thief. How dare you talk about him like that!"

"Where is he?" it sneered.

Kate yelled, "F, Y, I...I, D, K!"

"<u>F</u>or <u>Y</u>our <u>I</u>nformation <u>I</u> <u>D</u>on't <u>K</u>now," said the alien cat. "Hmm...I'll find out what you do know."

The alien cat turned off the dragonfly bleep. It leaped up using its claws trying to slash through the net.

It tried again, but this time Marvin kicked the alien cat in the head.

It fell to the ground. It did not move.

Kate yelled, "Yes!"

"Just call me '*Knock-out Foot*'," chuckled Marvin.

Kate stared at the alien cat looking for any sign that it was still alive. "Marvin! I hope it's not dead."

"Kate! It's okay. Look at its tail."

Kate stared at it. Yes, the tail was moving. The jewels on its collar changed from pink to red and started making a strange noise.

"It's some kind of tracking device," said Marvin.

Kate asked, "What do you mean?"

"Come on…don't you get it? It's calling for back-up."

"Oh, that's just great!" hissed Kate.

Kate slipped her fingers in the holes and tried to rip the material with her bare hands. "I want out!"

Chapter Four: The Hero

It was no use! The rough material was digging into Kate's fingers and she had to stop.

"We can't just sit here and wait for its buddies to show up," cried Kate.

"If I only had my backpack, I could have used the wire cutter," replied Marvin. "But, of course, I left it back at the tree house."

"What wire cutter?" asked Kate.

Marvin whispered, "An old one that Father keeps in his fishing box and doesn't use anymore."

"WHAT?" Kate said. "I can't believe you took it."

"Well," mumbled Marvin. "Like I said it's his old one. I was with him when he bought the new one."

"You should have asked him for the wire cutter, instead of just taking it," scolded Kate.

"You're right," Marvin said. "I should have asked him."

"Well, it doesn't make any difference," Kate whined. "Because…we're stuck here!"

Kate was about to say something else, when she heard a strange, clucking noise. Whatever it was began to mess with her hair. Kate reached up and grabbed something that was hairy and bony. It was an arm. The owner began to screech loudly.

"What in the world?" muttered Kate.

"Let it go," said Marvin. "It's that monkey."

Kate released the arm. The monkey was behind her. She could feel something wet dripping down her forehead.

"Is that monkey drooling on me?"

"Probably," chuckled Marvin. "It's trying to gnaw a hole through the net."

Kate reached up. She tried to grab the monkey again.

Marvin knocked her hand away. "Leave it alone! It's trying to help us."

The monkey kept gnawing until the hole was big enough.

Kate stuck her arm through it. She reached for one of the net's thick ropes hanging from a branch. Marvin lifted her up and she was able to get a firm grip. Kate climbed out. She kept going until she was in the tree.

Soon, the humming noise had stopped. Kate glanced over in the direction of the alien cat. The help squad had arrived. Three alien cats had formed a triangle around the injured one.

Kate and Marvin stayed hidden behind some branches watching the creatures down below. They began to think about their *little hero* when it suddenly appeared out of nowhere. Kate did not see it leap out of the tree. It was jumping on top of the gray alien cat.

The monkey hissed at the other three cats. They leaped and ran into each other. The monkey spat at them, before taking off.

Chapter Five: The Enemy

The alien cats chased after the monkey.

Kate whispered. "I can't believe the monkey did that!"

"Spit at the alien cats?" teased Marvin.

"You know what I mean!"

"Yes, it was a brave thing the monkey did," replied Marvin.

They were about to leave, when Kate heard a voice. It came from the alien cat.

The red jewels on the collar had turned back to pink. Kate noticed that the jewels were lit on the dragonfly bleep.

"Don't leave me."

Kate pointed at the alien cat. "It's asking for our help."

"Let's keep going! I didn't hear anything," mumbled Marvin.

Kate began walking towards it. "Well, I did!"

Marvin grabbed her arm. "Are you insane?"

Kate pulled away. "We have to help it."

Marvin reached for Kate again. "Oh, no, we don't!"

Kate knocked his hand away. "Yes, we do!"

"Please, help me! They won't come back. I'm all alone," said the alien cat.

Marvin walked with Kate. "Okay, I heard it that time."

They stood looking down at it, unsure of what to do.

"I can't believe it's hurt this bad. I only kicked it with my foot," said Marvin.

"Neither can I!" replied the alien cat.

When the alien cat opened its eyes and looked at Kate and Marvin, they took a few steps back.

"Don't be afraid! I'm not your enemy, but I know who is."

"Why are you lying to us?" Kate asked. "After all, you tried to attack us!"

"I was trying to set you free," replied the alien cat. "I wanted to protect you."

Marvin stepped closer to it. He looked down at the alien cat and asked, "Protect us from whom?"

The cat grinned. "Help me and I will tell you."

Marvin pulled Kate away from the alien creature. "Let's talk behind those bushes."

The bushes were far enough away, so they could talk without being overheard by the alien cat.

"I don't know what we should do," whispered Kate.

"We should just leave it. I'm sure its friends will come back," replied Marvin.

"I don't know," Kate swallowed. "What if it's telling the truth?"

"And what if it's not?" added Marvin.

Marvin took Kate's arm and began to drag her away. "We're wasting time! We should leave right now."

Kate almost gave in. But, then she heard the alien cat crying, "Help me...*please*."

Kate ran towards it. "Marvin, it's in pain."

Marvin reached the alien cat before Kate did. "We'll help you only if you tell us who our enemy is."

"Do you really want to know?" asked the alien cat.

"Yes," Kate said. "We want to know."

It stared at Kate with its yellow eyes. Kate gulped. She had a bad feeling about this.

"Tell us!" urged Marvin.

When the alien cat did not speak, Marvin began to walk away. "It's playing with us. It wants to keep us here until its friends return."

"Danger," said the alien cat. "Danger…is the enemy!"

What happens next in book 4 "Danger"?

The gray, alien cat claims that Danger should not be trusted. Is it possible that the alien cat is telling the truth? If so, what is the black alien dog really after? Read the next book, "Danger" to find out.

Suggestions for Using the Book, "Alien Cat"

After each chapter, students can provide oral or written predictions as to what they think will happen next.

After completing this book, challenge students to create an alternate ending.

Comprehension Check for Students

Another title for this book could be
    A.   The Dragonfly Bleep
    B.   The Green Net
    C.   Knuckle Brain
    D.   Monkey to the Rescue

Before the alien cat saw Kate and Marvin trapped inside the net,

    A.   the alien cat called Danger a thief.
    B.   Marvin kicked the alien cat in the head.
    C.   Kate wiped her hand on Marvin's pants.
    D.   a strange noise came from the alien cat's collar.

After Kate and Marvin got out of the net,

    A.   the monkey drooled on Kate.

    B.   three more alien cats appeared.

    C.   Kate heard a strange, clucking noise.

    D.   the monkey jumped on the alien cat.

Another word for 'device' is

    A.   collar

    B.   weapon

    C.   tool

    D.   bleep

At the end of the book, the alien cat asked for Kate and Marvin's help. More than likely,

    A.   the monkey will give the frog bleep to the alien cat.

    B.   the other three alien cats will return.

    C.   Marvin will stay with the alien cat while Kate goes for help.

    D.   Kate and Marvin will invite the alien cat to dinner.

About the Author

Sharon Oberne is the mother of Laura, Aaron, and Kelley and has a son-in-law named "Daric." She lives in Norfolk, Virginia with her husband, Ron, and their two cats, Goku and Peekaboo.

Mrs. Oberne is a literacy specialist working with young children. She believes in fostering creativity in children, because it opens the door to all possibilities.

Sharon is the founder of the national award winning, "After Breakfast Buddy Reading Club." She is the recipient of a Daily Point of Light Award from the Points of Light Foundation, the Grand-Prize Winner in Nickelodeon's Bright Orange Teacher Contest, Cox Cable's Educator of the Year, Teacher of the Year, among other recognitions.

Check out her website at:
www.readingisfunlibrary.com

DISGRACED!

The Dirty History of Performance-Enhancing Drugs in Sports™

MAJOR LEAGUE BASEBALL
The Great Steroid Scandals

JASON PORTERFIELD

rosen publishing's
rosen
central®

New York

Published in 2010 by The Rosen Publishing Group, Inc.
29 East 21st Street, New York, NY 10010

Library of Congress Cataloging-in-Publication Data

Porterfield, Jason.
Major league baseball: the great steroid scandals / Jason Porterfield.—1st ed.
    p. cm.—(Disgraced! the dirty history of performance-enhancing drugs in sports)
Includes bibliographical references and index.
ISBN-13: 978-1-4358-5302-7 (library binding)
1. Baseball—Corrupt practices—United States—Juvenile literature. 2. Baseball players—Drug use—United States—Juvenile literature. 3. Doping in sports—United States—Juvenile literature. I. Title.
GV877.5.P67 2010
796.3570973—dc22

                                                                            2008055581

Manufactured in the United States of America

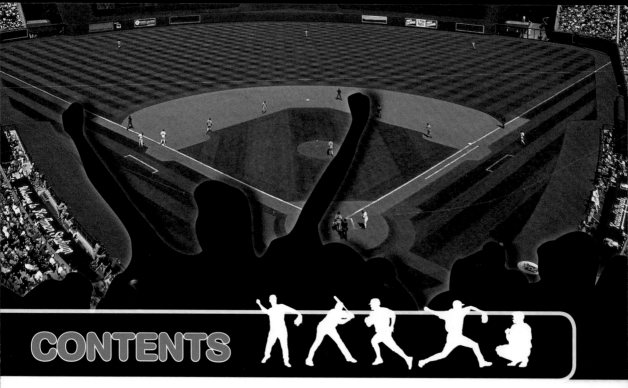

CONTENTS

Introduction

To win in baseball, players must be able to hit, run, pitch, and field the ball better than their opponents. The hardest-working players take endless batting practice and spend countless hours perfecting their fielding and throwing skills. Most have workout regimens to keep themselves fit. Many even play winter ball as a way of keeping their skills sharp for the next season. Pitchers watch footage of particular hitters to get a feel for which pitches to throw and which to avoid. Hitters, for their part, watch video of pitchers to see what they are likely to pitch in particular situations. Playing baseball, in other words, requires hard work and patience. A player vows to become stronger, faster, or more agile, and he works diligently to accomplish his goal. Some players, however, decide that they can't get results fast enough through hard work alone. Or they feel that even after training hard, they still aren't as good at the game as they feel they should be. These players may turn to performance-enhancing drugs, such as steroids or human growth hormone, to get the results they desire.

Major League Baseball (MLB) has banned performance-enhancing drugs, but that hasn't stopped players from using them. Those who do use them may say they only want to help their team win. But, unfortunately, these players are damaging their bodies, their reputations, and the legacy of the game.

Former Philadelphia Phillies catcher Bobby Estalella flexes his muscles during spring training in 1998. In 2007, Estalella was named in the Mitchell Report as one of the major leaguers who had used performance-enhancing drugs.

Baseball's Steroid Explosion

Today, the most serious concerns about performance-enhancing drugs in baseball are related to steroids. But steroids are hardly the first performance enhancers used in the sport.

Baseball and Amphetamines

Amphetamine pills have been used in baseball since the 1940s. Amphetamines are drugs designed to stimulate the nervous system, with the result of increasing alertness. They were originally marketed to the public in the 1930s in the form of an inhaler that was sold under the brand name Benzedrine. Not knowing the long-term effects of the drugs, medical professionals came to recommend amphetamines to treat a host of conditions.

During the 1940s, baseball players who had fought in World War II introduced amphetamines to the sport with tales of how the drugs had helped them stay awake and alert for days. Players began taking them to improve their alertness at the plate and in the field. The drugs also helped them endure the grind of the long baseball season.

Amphetamine pills, known as "greenies," became extremely common in baseball clubhouses during the 1950s and 1960s, even as the negative side effects of the drugs became better known. Baseball's attitude toward amphetamines was lax. Team officials often looked the other way as their star players took the

In 2006, baseball's all-time career hits leader Pete Rose told television host David Letterman that he took "greenies" during his playing days "to lose some weight." Rose is shown here in the 1960s making his trademark headfirst slide.

drugs. In the book *The Juice: The Real Story of Baseball's Drug Problems*, sports journalist Will Carroll and athletic trainer and educator William L. Carroll write that amphetamines were openly dispensed in baseball clubhouses by the 1960s. During the infamous "Pittsburgh Drug Trials" of 1985, former players John Milner, Dave Parker, and Dale Berra testified that superstars Willie Mays and Willie Stargell, both now members of the Baseball Hall of Fame, used amphetamines. Greenies remained part of baseball for decades, and the sport didn't take strong measures to halt their use until 2005, when a new drug policy was formulated.

During the Pittsburgh Drug Trials, All-Star outfielder Tim Raines admitted to using the illegal stimulant cocaine. Raines, shown here playing for the Montreal Expos, managed to quit the drug, completing his long career in 2002.

Baseball's Cocaine Problem

During the 1970s and 1980s, some players turned to cocaine as a way to artificially improve their play. (At the same time, cocaine's use as a party drug was also increasing.) Players used cocaine before and during games for the same reasons they used amphetamines, believing that the drug could help them stay alert and improve their reaction time. Some players continued to use cocaine even after pitcher Ferguson Jenkins was briefly banned for life from baseball in 1980, following his arrest for possession of the drug. Jenkins was reinstated in 1981 and elected to the Hall of Fame in 1991, but the suspension likely delayed his election.

By the mid-1980s, it became clear that baseball's cocaine problem was widespread. Sports journalist Ron Cook, writing in the *Pittsburgh Post-Gazette* in September 2000, told how, in 1985, seven players were summoned before a grand jury in Pittsburgh, Pennsylvania, to testify about drug use in the major leagues. These players included All-Stars Tim Raines, Dave Parker, and Keith Hernandez. Their testimony led to the so-called Pittsburgh Drug Trials and cast suspicion on many players on the Pittsburgh Pirates team that won the 1979 World Series. Several drug dealers were also involved in the case, including a man who served as a mascot for the Pirates team.

In February 1986, Peter Ueberroth, the commissioner of baseball at the time, suspended eleven players for their drug use. Ueberroth made it mandatory for the suspended players to perform community service before they could be reinstated (allowed to play again). The original agreement also called for the reinstated players to submit to regular drug testing for the remainder of their careers. However, the players' union, which represents players in their dealings with baseball administrators, successfully fought that measure.

In spite of the suspensions, cocaine use continued. Hall of Fame member Paul Molitor, who was not one of the suspended players, ultimately succeeded in quitting the drug. Other stars, including outfielder Darryl Strawberry and pitcher Steve Howe, had their careers derailed by drug problems. In 1992, Howe became the second player ever to be banned for life from baseball due to drug abuse. He was reinstated in 1993 but was never able to fully overcome his drug problems. He retired from baseball in 1996 and was killed in a car accident in 2006.

The Redemption of Dock Ellis

During the 1970s, Dock Ellis was one of baseball's rising stars. A fierce and controversial competitor, Ellis frequently intimidated batters with his notorious "brush-back" pitches. In June 2005, *Dallas Observer* sportswriter Keven McAlester wrote that Ellis admitted to using amphetamines during his career. He also said that he developed a serious cocaine addiction near the end of his career. Fortunately, Ellis was able to turn his life around, kicking his drug problem and becoming a substance abuse counselor at a corrections facility in California.

Steroids Come to Baseball

Since the late 1980s and early 1990s, steroids have been the focus of the performance-enhancing drugs issue. Steroids are a class of drugs that includes many substances designed to increase strength and muscle mass. Anabolic, or muscle-building, steroids were first widely produced in the 1940s and 1950s. Athletes in sports like weight lifting, bodybuilding, and wrestling have abused steroids for decades. Use of the drugs in baseball, however, didn't become noticeable until the 1980s. By the late 1980s, it seemed that even normal-size players were hitting impressive home runs at an unusual clip. By the 1990s, the trend was unmistakable. In 1996, for example, seventeen players hit 40 or more home runs. The previous high, set in 1961, was 8.

One of the major problems stemming from baseball's era of steroid scandals is the question of how history will view players who had outstanding years during this time. Orioles' outfielder Brady Anderson is a prime example.

Before the 1980s, steroid use was common among bodybuilders and weight lifters, but not so widespread in baseball.

Throughout his career, Anderson kept in top physical shape with a specialized diet and a rigorous exercise regimen. In addition, he was considered one of the major leagues' top lead-off hitters. In 1996, however, Anderson smacked a surprising 50 home runs. His previous season high had been 21 home runs, in 1992. After 1996, his next highest home run total was 24, in 1999. Anderson denied ever using steroids and was never named as a user in any legal cases. Nevertheless, his accomplishments in 1996 may forever be tainted by the rumors of rampant steroid use that plagued the era.

At first, Major League Baseball did little to address the steroid issue. The league added steroids to a list of banned substances in 1991, but there was no provision calling for players to be tested for the drugs.

The 1998 Home Run Race: Excitement Mixed with Suspicion

In 1998, Mark McGwire of the St. Louis Cardinals and Sammy Sosa of the Chicago Cubs made history. Both sluggers broke Roger Maris's single-season record of 61 home runs, set in 1961. McGwire established the new record by finishing the season with 70 homers, while Sosa hit 66. After Maris and Babe Ruth, McGwire and Sosa became just the third and fourth players in major league history to hit more than 60 home runs. The two were hailed as heroes and credited with reawakening the public's interest in baseball. For good measure, the following season, 1999, McGwire and Sosa hit 65 and 63 home runs, respectively.

Both Sosa and McGwire were muscular, and they attributed their bulk to exercise. Though McGwire had always been big, Sosa started his baseball career as a slender and speedy outfielder. According to a *New York Times* article published August 27, 1998, McGwire admitted to using the performance enhancer androstenedione during his record-breaking season. It's a prohormone, or a chemical that helps the body produce hormones. Androstenedione was not banned at the time. Both players eventually hit more than 500 home runs in their careers, and Sosa became just the fifth player ever to hit more than 600 home runs, in 2007. However, their later careers were slowed by chronic injuries, and their suspected steroid use diminished them in the eyes of many fans.

In 2001, San Francisco Giants outfielder Barry Bonds finished the season with 73 homers, surpassing McGwire's mark. Bonds had long been considered one of the best players in baseball, with a rare combination of speed and power. By 2001, he had developed a large, muscular physique, which he attributed to hours spent training in the gym. Unlike McGwire and Sosa, however, Bonds had a reputation as a moody player who often clashed with the media.

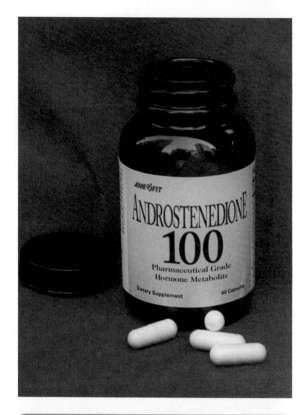

Pro athletes like Mark McGwire used the dietary supplement androstenedione to increase their strength.

The public quickly became suspicious of Bonds's home run totals. Maris's record had stood for thirty-seven years before McGwire broke it, whereas McGwire's record lasted only three seasons before Bonds broke it. Bonds denied using performance-enhancing drugs, but the rumors persisted, and many fans turned away from him. Bonds broke Hank Aaron's career home run record in 2007, but fans failed to express the admiration that they might have afforded someone else. When the 2008 season began, no team was willing to place Bonds on its roster. And, in 2009, evidence was released that appeared to link Bonds to positive tests for steroids and other performance-enhancing drugs. This evidence may provide proof that Bonds had committed perjury, or lied while under oath, during a federal grand jury trial. At this trial, which took place in 2003, Bonds had testified that he'd never consciously used performance-enhancing drugs.

From 2001 to the end of 2008, no other player reached the 60-home-run plateau, but home run totals did remain high. Before 1990, only ten players had

Plaques honoring baseball's greatest players hang in the Baseball Hall of Fame in Cooperstown, New York. It remains to be seen if known steroid users will be inducted into the hall.

ever hit 50 or more home runs in a season. Since 1990, however, fifteen players have accomplished the feat. Smaller ballparks, livelier baseballs, a decline in pitching talent, and the exercise regimens of modern players have all been cited as possible factors in the offensive explosion. Of course, after McGwire's use of androstenedione was made public, steroids also became part of the mix.

Drug Testing Begins

In 2003, players were tested for amphetamines for the first time. The test results were to be kept secret, and players who tested positive were not to be punished.

Major League Baseball stepped up testing in 2006. Each player on a major league team roster was tested at least twice, with approximately six hundred other tests conducted randomly. With random in-season testing, players are selected by chance to undergo testing during the season. Random in-season testing is intended to catch players who stop using drugs during spring training, when scheduled tests are performed, and start using again when the season begins.

If a player tested positive in 2006, the test results were to remain confidential. But the player would have to submit to more testing and treatment. A second positive test would result in a twenty-five-game suspension. Players testing positive for a third time would be suspended for eighty games. Even harsher penalties were put in place in 2007.

Though the 2006 test results were supposed to remain confidential, both the *New York Daily News* and *USA Today* newspapers reported that sluggers Barry Bonds of the San Francisco Giants and Jason Giambi of the New York Yankees had tested positive for amphetamines. Both players tested positive only once, but the incident damaged their reputations. Coincidentally, both had also been the subjects of widespread rumors of steroid use.

Chapter 2

Unmasking the Users

I n 2002, just a year after San Francisco Giants star Barry Bonds broke the single-season home run record, former major league player Ken Caminiti revealed to Tom Verducci of *Sports Illustrated* magazine that he had used steroids during his career. The span of his steroid use included 1996, the year he was named the National League's Most Valuable Player (MVP). "It's no secret what's going on in baseball," Caminiti told Verducci. "At least half the players are using steroids."

Ken Caminiti died of a heart attack in 2004 in New York City, where the medical examiner found a combination of cocaine and opiates in his system. Caminiti was also found to have had an enlarged heart, possibly caused by his steroid use.

The Case of BALCO

Bonds had a personal trainer named Greg Anderson, who worked with the Bay Area Laboratory Co-operative (BALCO). In 2003, a federal grand jury formally charged Anderson with providing steroids to athletes. The court agreed to conceal the names of the athletes involved in the investigation, but their testimony was leaked. It was soon revealed that the BALCO case involved Bonds and New York Yankees first baseman Jason Giambi.

In his testimony, Bonds flatly denied that he knowingly used steroids. Giambi, a former MVP for the Oakland Athletics, admitted to steroid use in his

Ken Caminiti, shown here playing for the Houston Astros in 2000, was one of the first major league stars—and the first high-profile player—to admit to steroid use.

testimony before the grand jury. The information was reported in the *San Francisco Chronicle* by Mark Fainaru-Wada and Lance Williams. The writers later expanded their coverage of steroid use into the book *Game of Shadows: Barry Bonds, BALCO, and the Steroids Scandal That Rocked Professional Sports.*

The federal investigation that began with the 2003 BALCO raid raised questions about the effectiveness of U.S. laws against performance-enhancing drugs. (These laws are commonly known as anti-doping laws.) The BALCO case

Victor Conte founded the Bay Area Laboratory Co-operative (BALCO) in 1984. The company's headquarters *(above)* were located in Burlingame, California, south of San Francisco.

touched prominent athletes in many sports, particularly baseball, football, and track and field. According to *Game of Shadows*, during his grand jury testimony, BALCO client Giambi allegedly stated that he hadn't worried about testing because he used steroids only during the off-season. The fallout from the BALCO scandal also resulted in criminal perjury charges for Bonds, who was accused of lying under oath when he denied knowingly taking steroids.

Others involved in BALCO have already served time in jail, including Greg Anderson and BALCO owner Victor Conte. Both pleaded guilty to charges of steroid distribution and other charges, and each served several months in prison. After completing his sentence in early 2006, Anderson returned to prison twice more on contempt charges for refusing to testify against Bonds.

More Rumors and Accusations

Players and former players fueled the steroid discussion in statements to the media and by making allegations in their own books. For example, in his 2005 autobiography, *Juiced: Wild Times, Rampant 'Roids, Smash Hits, and How Baseball Got Big*, former baseball player José Canseco admitted to steroid use. The one-time Rookie of the Year and MVP award winner also singled out several other prominent players as users, including McGwire, Giambi, Bonds, and Baltimore Orioles slugger Rafael Palmeiro. The book spurred the U.S. government to hold hearings in March 2005 to investigate steroid abuse in baseball.

Seven prominent baseball players—Giambi, Sosa, Palmeiro, two-time MVP Frank Thomas, All-Star pitcher Curt Schilling, and former players Canseco and McGwire—were called to appear before the U.S. Congress. Baseball commissioner Bud Selig, who oversees MLB operations, and Donald Fehr of the players' union also appeared. As a result of the hearings, Congress appointed former senator George Mitchell to serve as a special investigator into allegations of baseball's steroid use.

Of the players who appeared before Congress, only Giambi and Canseco had ever admitted publicly to using steroids. Schilling and Thomas had long been outspoken critics of the drugs, while Palmeiro and Sosa denied using steroids. The most surprising testimony came from slugger Mark McGwire, who had retired from baseball in 2001. When asked under oath about steroid use,

In March 2005, Rafael Palmeiro denied using performance-enhancing drugs in his testimony before members of Congress. Less than six months later, Palmeiro tested positive for steroids.

McGwire declined to answer. His actions disappointed fans, many of whom took his silence as an admission of guilt.

Steroid Testing

As part of a new Joint Drug Treatment and Prevention Program, Major League Baseball began random testing for steroids in 2003. However, the results were

kept confidential, and there were no penalties. More than 5 percent of test samples taken that season came back positive, so anonymous tests were performed again in 2004. After the congressional hearings, however, more severe penalties were put into place. Beginning in 2005, if a player tested positive, he would be suspended for ten games for the first offense, thirty for the second, and sixty for the third. If he tested positive a fourth time, he would be suspended for one year.

Twelve major league players tested positive for steroids and received suspensions during the 2005 season. Among them was Palmeiro, who had vehemently denied using steroids when he testified before Congress. Reports of his positive test, for the anabolic steroid stanozolol, were published by the *New York Times* on August 3, 2005. Shortly after returning from his ten-day suspension, his team, the Baltimore Orioles, benched him. Palmeiro hasn't played since.

Before the 2006 season began, Major League Baseball and the players' union bowed to pressure from Congress and agreed to in-season testing for steroid use, as well as tougher penalties for getting caught. Players testing positive are now suspended fifty games for a first offense and a hundred games for a second. They are banned from baseball for life after a third positive test. Between 2006 and 2008, at least twenty major league players were suspended for using steroids.

The Grimsley Raid

During the 2006 season, federal agents raided the home of Jason Grimsley, after the Arizona Diamondbacks pitcher received a shipment of human growth hormone (HGH) through the mail. In his home, investigators found information on a broad network of people dealing in performance-enhancing drugs. Most were involved in selling steroids and HGH. According to an article written by Lance Williams and published in the December 21, 2007, *San Francisco Chronicle*, Grimsley acknowledged that he had used amphetamines, HGH, and steroids, and he agreed to cooperate with the investigation that followed. Arizona suspended him for fifty games but released him from his contract before he served the suspension. Grimsley then retired and has not played since.

Grimsley played for several different teams during his career. During the investigation, he named prominent players on different teams who he claimed

George Mitchell

George Mitchell served as a senator from Maine from 1980 to 1995. He has long been respected for his mediation work in ending conflicts, both while serving in the Senate and in his private life since leaving politics. However, his role as the primary investigator into drug use in baseball has been criticized because he worked for the Boston Red Sox and holds a small ownership stake in the team. Mitchell responded to these criticisms by saying that the report showed no favoritism to the Red Sox.

had used performance-enhancing drugs. These included former American League MVP Miguel Tejada, along with former players José Canseco, Glenallen Hill, David Seguí, Lenny Dykstra, and Chuck Knoblauch.

The Mitchell Report

By 2006, some members of Congress were becoming frustrated with the pace of Major League Baseball's attempt to end the use of performance-enhancing drugs. Bud Selig, the commissioner of baseball, eventually appointed former senator George Mitchell to lead an independent investigation into the use of performance-enhancing drugs in baseball.

Mitchell's investigation took twenty months to complete. It focused on the actions of individual players, without investigating the role that teams may

In January 2008, baseball commissioner Bud Selig (with hands on mouth) shows the strain of undergoing a Congressional inquiry into his organization. Senator George Mitchell listens in the foreground.

have played. According to Mitchell, the players' union was uncooperative and discouraged individual players from cooperating. More than seven hundred people were interviewed for the report, including more than sixty former players and two active players, Frank Thomas and Jason Giambi. Team managers, coaches, physicians, athletic trainers, security personnel, and team officials were also interviewed. Teams and the commissioner's office provided the investigation with more than 115,000 pages of documents and 2,000 electronic documents.

February 13, 2008—Roger Clemens is sworn in prior to testifying before Congress. One of the most successful pitchers ever, Clemens was linked to steroid use in the Mitchell Report.

The investigation resulted in the four-hundred-page Mitchell Report. Released in December 2007, the report covers the history of performance-enhancing drugs in baseball, as well as the effectiveness of Major League Baseball's Joint Drug Prevention and Treatment Program. The report also investigates the status of baseball players as role models. It notes, for example, that after McGwire admitted to using androstenedione in 1998, sales of the supplement climbed by more than 1,000 percent.

The report named about ninety players, past and present, from all thirty MLB teams, who had allegedly used performance-enhancing drugs. This group included stars Andy Pettitte, Miguel Tejada, and Eric Gagne. The list included thirty-one former All-Stars and eight former MVPs, such as sluggers Barry Bonds, Ken Caminiti, Juan González, Mo Vaughn, Matt Williams, and David Justice. It included star pitchers Kevin Brown and Denny Neagle. Two days after the Mitchell Report was issued, Pettitte held a news conference in which he confessed to trying HGH for two days while recovering from an elbow injury in 2002. Many other current players either denied using steroids or remained silent on the issue. Pettitte and others returned to play during the 2008 season. One prominent player not mentioned in the report was Mark McGwire.

One of the biggest names in the report was Roger Clemens. Clemens had been one of baseball's top pitchers since the mid-1980s. He was considered by many to be one of the best pitchers of all time, having won seven Cy Young Awards throughout his career. At the end of the 2007 season, he ranked ninth all-time with 354 wins and third all-time with 4,672 strikeouts. In the Mitchell Report, former Yankees trainer Brian McNamee, who served as a personal strength coach for both Clemens and Pettitte, claimed he had injected Clemens with the steroid Winstrol during the 1998, 2000, and 2001 seasons. Later, Clemens publicly denied the allegations and filed a defamation suit against McNamee, but he has not played baseball since the report was released.

Chapter 3

The Effects of Steroids

Many people, when they think of performance-enhancing drugs, immediately think of steroids. "Steroids" is a somewhat vague term, though. Steroids are actually a broad class of chemicals naturally produced by the body. For example, your body releases its own steroids called corticosteroids to control inflammation and swelling.

Anabolic Steroids

Testosterone, the male sex hormone, is a type of steroid. The specific agents used by athletes are forms of steroids related to male sex hormones, called anabolic-androgenic steroids. The ones in use today are synthetic: they have been created in a laboratory. More than a hundred different anabolic steroids have been developed.

Anabolic steroids have both anabolic and androgenic effects. The anabolic effects result in increased muscle mass. Androgenic, or masculinizing, effects may include a deeper voice and increased growth of body hair. Athletes use steroids for the anabolic effects, but these cannot be separated from the androgenic effects.

Anabolic steroids are best known for their use in boosting physical performance. They also have some medical uses. For example, doctors prescribe anabolic steroids in hormone replacement therapy, to treat the effects of

Burly slugger Mark McGwire captured the nation's attention when he broke Roger Maris's single-season home run record in 1998. Since then, rumors of McGwire's steroid use have tarnished his reputation.

certain diseases including AIDS (acquired immunodeficiency syndrome) and some forms of cancer, and to induce puberty in boys who are slow to develop. Anabolic steroids have also been manufactured for veterinary use. Athletes have abused these steroids, too.

Athletes using illicit steroids can take them orally, in the form of a tablet or capsule, or can inject them into muscle. They can also apply some steroids to the skin in the form of a cream or ointment. Users often "stack," or combine

different steroids to maximize the effect or to avoid detection. Users' carefully designed regimens usually last from about a month to three months. Typical doses are huge, up to sixty times larger than doses prescribed for medical purposes.

Although steroids bulk up muscle mass, they do not increase strength. In order to benefit from the increased muscle, steroid users must also do resistance training. Players using steroids are able to work out harder and avoid the muscle fatigue that would occur without steroid use.

Steroid Side Effects

Steroids change the balance of the body's hormones, chemicals that affect the way the body functions. This change in balance may cause a variety of side effects. Both men and women may experience such changes as increased growth of body hair, male-pattern baldness, and a deeper voice. These symptoms are some-times irreversible. Men may experience shrinkage of the testes and develop enlarged breasts, a result of some testosterone being converted into the female sex hormone estradiol.

Since players often lie about their steroid use, it is difficult for researchers to gauge the full extent of the long-term and short-term side effects on heavy, habitual steroid users. It is known, however, that the drugs' dangerous side effects can cause permanent damage or even be fatal. Even young, otherwise healthy athletes are at risk. Many users injure tendons and ligaments, which are not able to support the unnaturally enlarged muscles. Steroids can affect blood cholesterol levels and trigger cardiovascular diseases like heart attack, stroke, and an enlarged heart. They can damage the liver, which processes the drugs once they enter the body. Users may develop liver disease including hepatitis, hepatic cancer (tumors), or cysts. The kidneys, prostate (in men), and reproductive system may also suffer adverse effects. Adolescents using steroids risk stunting their height, as high levels of testosterone can fool the body into triggering a premature end to bone growth.

The psychological side effects of steroid use can be significant, too. Some researchers claim that steroids make users more aggressive, a condition known as "'roid rage." Studies have not been able to prove without a doubt that

The Major League Baseball Players Association

The Major League Baseball Players Association is a labor union. The organization was created in 1966 to look after the interests of players and especially to make sure that player contracts and salaries meet the union's standards.

In the past, the union fought against drug screening for players. However, negative publicity following the **BALCO** case helped convince many players to drop their opposition to testing.

anabolic steroids cause violent outbursts, but it is widely acknowledged that steroid use is linked with an increased risk of severe mood swings, manic behavior, and depression. Some researchers also believe that steroids are psychologically addictive. In other words, the user's body isn't dependent on the drugs, but the user's mind is tricked into believing that the drug is necessary in order to perform well.

Human Growth Hormone (HGH)

Human growth hormone (HGH) is different from anabolic steroids but can be abused as a performance enhancer. Naturally produced by the pituitary gland, HGH stimulates growth during childhood and adolescence. Synthetic HGH was developed to treat patients with conditions like hormone deficiency. Athletes and others are sometimes prescribed HGH or related compounds to promote

During his 2003 testimony in the BALCO case, Jason Giambi admitted to using steroids and human growth hormone. The drugs may have contributed to health problems, including a pituitary tumor that plagued him during the 2004 season.

muscle development and cartilage growth to help them recover from injuries. Unfortunately, athletes also take HGH illegally—usually in combination with steroids—thinking it will increase their strength, stamina, and power.

Adverse side effects of taking HGH include abnormal growth of bones in the face and enlargement of the liver or other organs. Use of HGH to enhance performance is a fairly new phenomenon, so little is known about long-term effects. Since it's produced naturally in the body, HGH is very hard to detect through drug tests. While there are still no reliable tests for the drug, it has been placed on Major League Baseball's banned substances list. The Mitchell Report

focused primarily on steroids, but it also addressed the growing use of HGH among players. The report concluded that when random steroid testing began in 2003, players began turning to HGH as a way to get around the tests.

Testing in Baseball

Individual players and the players' union have been wary of drug testing since the fallout from the Pittsburgh Drug Trials. After all, testing for drugs implies suspicion. Furthermore, some feel that testing is an invasion of privacy. However, baseball officials are concerned that the game's image could be forever tarnished if the use of steroids and other performance-enhancing drugs becomes wide-spread. Inevitably, both sides had to make compromises in order to pass a testing agreement.

Today, dozens of different drugs are on MLB's banned substances list. This number includes drugs of abuse, such as marijuana and cocaine; about fifty different steroids; human growth hormone; and thirty distinct amphetamines. Players are currently tested through urine samples. These are taken during spring training and again at the beginning of the season. They may also be taken randomly during the season. Urine tests can confirm the use of most substances on baseball's banned substances list. However, they are not as reliable as other, more invasive tests, such as testing blood and hair samples. In addition, players may take legal supplements to mask their use of performance-enhancing drugs. The masking agents are more effective in urine tests than in blood or hair tests. Players using performance-enhancing drugs may also find a way to submit someone else's untainted urine to the testers and thus avoid getting caught.

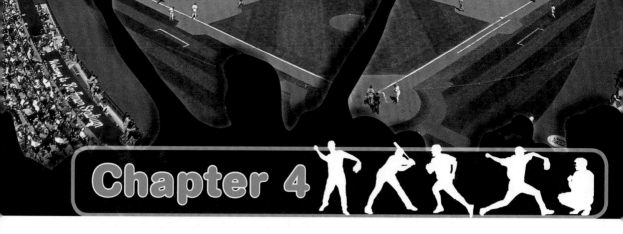

Chapter 4

Tainted Legacies

San Francisco Giants outfielder Barry Bonds won seven National League Most Valuable Player awards during his career and helped lead the Giants to the World Series in 2002. On August 7, 2007, he hit his 756th career home run, breaking a record that Hank Aaron had held for thirty-three years. Despite the slugger's accomplishments with the team, the Giants cut ties with Bonds after the 2007 season.

He did not play baseball in 2008. Some speculated that teams weren't willing to pay the high salary that the aging player would command, or they didn't want to deal with his often-surly personality in the clubhouse. Others suspected that teams simply didn't want to be linked in any way to Bonds while he faces perjury charges for his testimony in the BALCO case. Some fans hailed his achievement in breaking Hank Aaron's record, but others felt that the new record was tainted by the steroid allegations.

Other players linked to steroid use have faced similar scorn from fans. Palmeiro served a ten-day suspension for testing positive for steroids in 2005. When he returned to the playing field, he was so bothered by the fans' loud booing that he had to wear earplugs to play. When McGwire first became eligible for election to the Hall of Fame in 2006, he received less than 25 percent of the ballots. (At least 75 percent is needed for someone to be elected.) Many attributed his low vote total to a backlash caused by his performance before Congress in 2005. Both McGwire and Palmeiro had been popular players,

Barry Bonds has hit more home runs than any other player in major league history, but his legacy may be tainted by his ties to the BALCO steroid case.

frequently mentioned as candidates for the Hall of Fame. However, their link to steroids may make it impossible for them to get inducted into the hall.

Why Players Cheat

Most athletes know about the negative consequences of using performance-enhancing drugs. The health risks of steroids and other doping agents have been well publicized. In addition to the physical consequences to the individual, there are other negative consequences to the entire sport of baseball.

The Asterisk Ball

In September 2007, businessman Marc Ecko paid $752,467 for the baseball that Barry Bonds hit for his record-breaking 756th home run. Ecko then set up a Web site, giving fans a chance to vote on the ball's fate. Depending on fan voting, Ecko would either send the ball to the Hall of Fame, brand the ball with an asterisk to symbolize the belief that Bonds cheated to break the record before sending it to the hall, or launch the ball into space. Fans overwhelmingly voted to have the ball branded with an asterisk. Ecko had the ball marked with an asterisk and he donated it to the Hall of Fame, where it is on display.

Players who choose to take drugs to improve their performance risk driving fans away, if they are caught. To millions of fans, baseball players are role models or heroes. They also serve as fans' own personal connections to the sport—when the player succeeds, fans of the player succeed, too. So when these larger-than-life figures are exposed as drug users, the entire sport is diminished in the eyes of many fans. What's more, when young players see evidence showing that many professionals use steroids, they get the message that cheating and drug use are acceptable behaviors.

What makes players decide that the advantages of performance-enhancing drugs outweigh the risks? Part of the incentive is money. The average salary in the MLB is more than $3 million a year, and top players have annual salaries in excess of $20 million a year. Players can make even more money from lucrative endorsement deals for everything from sports gear to cereal. With so much

Many baseball fans were dismayed when Barry Bonds eclipsed Hank Aaron's career home run record. Signs like this one suggested that fans did not view Bonds's achievement as equal to Aaron's.

money at stake, it's easy to see why a veteran player might consider taking steroids and other drugs as a way to extend a career, or as a way to come back after an injury. At the same time, an ambitious younger athlete may view performance-enhancing drugs as his best chance to break into the major leagues.

As the record shows, even good players are not immune to the temptation. The authors of *Game of Shadows* point to the 1998 home run race between McGwire and Sosa as a factor in Bonds's decision to start taking performance-enhancing drugs. Bonds had always been an excellent player, and he was often talked about as being one of the best ever. But he had never been embraced by fans in the same way that McGwire and Sosa had.

Andy Pettitte leaves congressional hearings in 2008. He admitted to using HGH.

It is easy to condemn individual athletes for their actions, but there is considerable pressure in the world of Major League Baseball to succeed at any cost. Fans are eager to see players set records and compete against one another in high-suspense games. In an age in which physical enhancements like cosmetic surgery and Botox injections are mainstream, players often feel that they must take whatever steps possible to mask any physical limitations or keep up with younger, stronger players. Also, if the use of performance-enhancing drugs is believed to be widespread in a sport, an athlete may feel that he or she has no choice but to turn to them to compete with other drug-enhanced athletes. For instance, even superstar Alex Rodriguez, the highest-paid player in baseball, confessed to using performance-enhancing drugs. In a February 9, 2009, interview with ESPN reporter Peter Gammons, Rodriguez said, "I was young. I was stupid. I was naive. And I wanted to prove to everyone that, you know, I was worth being one of the greatest players of all times. And I did take a banned substance. You know, for that I'm very sorry and deeply regretful."

Players may look at accepted and legal medical treatments as justification for using steroids. Today, the once-radical ligament replacement surgery named after former pitcher Tommy John has extended the careers of many pitchers since the surgery was first performed in 1974. Players can now treat creaky and painful joints with cortisone shots, and many players have had laser surgery to

Following a raid, U.S. Drug Enforcement Administration officers spread out vials of confiscated steroids. The federal agency works to shut down the production and distribution of illegal steroids in the United States.

correct their vision so that they can see the ball better. Some may wonder: if these measures are acceptable, why not use steroids, too?

Team owners, managers, and fans also add to the pressure to perform. In some circumstances, desperate players in high-pressure situations may resort to using steroids or other drugs to fulfill these expectations. This is particularly true for the injured player, who worries that he may be unable to regain his old form or that the team may replace him with a healthier player. Veteran pitcher Andy Pettitte, for example, confessed to using HGH while recovering from an elbow injury. Major League Baseball will make exceptions for players with a

legitimate medical need for drugs that are otherwise banned from the sport, but Pettitte did not have a prescription for HGH.

The Future of Performance-Enhancing Drugs in Baseball

Baseball's anti-doping policy has become tougher than what it was, but its policy is far less strict than that of other sports. Players caught for a first performance-enhancing drug offense are suspended for fifty games. These offenses include the nonprescription use of steroids and HGH. Since the new policy took effect prior to the 2006 season, suspended players include New York Mets reliever Guillermo Mota and Philadelphia Phillies' 2008 World Series hero J. C. Romero. They will be suspended for one hundred games if they're caught again and banned for life if they test positive for a third time.

Regarding illegal stimulant use, a player caught for the first time must undergo evaluation and follow-up testing. Subsequent positive tests for stimulants carry suspensions of twenty-five games, eighty games, and up to a lifetime ban. As of January 2009, only one major league player has received an eighty-game suspension. As the Associated Press reported on August 4, 2007, Detroit Tigers infielder Neifi Perez became the first three-time stimulant offender when he failed a test late in the 2007 season. If Perez tests positive again, the commissioner of baseball has the option to ban him from the game for life.

Major League Baseball is working to eliminate performance-enhancing drugs from the game, but loopholes still allow players to abuse some of them. (HGH is an example.) In addition, the dopers are often one step ahead of the regulators. For the players willing to risk their health and careers, steroid manufacturers will constantly work to find new ways to beat the current drug tests. In the BALCO case, for instance, federal investigators were told that an oral testosterone was available to players that could be undetectable within a week of discontinuing use. Use of such drugs, if in existence, likely would be very tricky for regulators to detect and punish.

GLOSSARY

amphetamines Group of drugs that act as stimulants of the central nervous system.

anabolic Describing a type of steroid that builds up muscles.

cardiovascular Related to the heart and blood vessels.

cartilage Tough, elastic connective tissue found in the joints and other parts of the body.

corticosteroids Steroid hormones naturally produced by the body.

diligently Steadily; earnestly and without tiring.

doping Another term for the use of performance-enhancing drugs.

endurance Stamina; in athletics, especially, the ability to perform certain types of exercise for long periods.

habitual Established by long use.

hormone Substance produced by the body that regulates functions, including growth and metabolism.

human growth hormone (HGH) Hormone secreted by the pituitary gland that promotes growth of the body.

illicit Illegal or unauthorized.

stamina Strength of physical constitution.

steroids (anabolic-androgenic steroids, or AAS) Class of hormones that promote growth, particularly of muscle and bone.

synthetic Produced artificially by humans.

tendon Cord of tough, inelastic tissue that connects muscle and bone.

testosterone A male sex hormone.

FOR MORE INFORMATION

Drug Enforcement Administration (DEA)
8701 Morrissette Drive
Springfield, VA 22152
(202) 307-7936
Web site: http://www.usdoj.gov/dea/index.htm
The DEA enforces the drug laws of the United States and prosecutes those who
  manufacture and distribute controlled substances, including steroids.

Major League Baseball
Office of the Commissioner of Baseball
245 Park Avenue, 31st floor
New York, NY 10167
(212) 931-7800
Web site. http://www.mlb.com
The Commissioner of Baseball's office oversees all aspects of Major League
  Baseball.

Major League Baseball Players' Union
12 East 49th Street, 24th Floor
New York, NY 10017
(212) 826-0808
Web site: http://mlbplayers.mlb.com
The Major League Baseball Players' Union is a group representing the interests of
  current and past major league players.

National Baseball Hall of Fame
25 Main Street
Cooperstown, NY 13326
(888) 425-5633

Web site: http://www.baseballhalloffame.org
The National Baseball Hall of Fame honors the game's greatest figures and most historic moments.

National Center for Drug Free Sport, Inc.
2537 Madison Avenue
Kansas City, MO 64108
(816) 474-8655
Web site: http://www.drugfreesport.com
This organization is dedicated to eliminating performance-enhancing drugs from sports.

National Institutes of Health
9000 Rockville Pike
Bethesda, MD 20892
(301) 496-4000
Web site: http://www.nih.gov
The National Institutes of Health is at the forefront of health-related research in the United States.

U.S. Anti-Doping Agency (USADA)
1330 Quail Lake Loop, Suite 260
Colorado Springs, CO 80906-4651
(866) 601-2632 or (719) 785-2000
Web site: http://www.usantidoping.org
The USADA is a national organization for policing doping in sports.

World Anti-Doping Agency (WADA)
Stock Exchange Tower

800 Place Victoria, Suite 1700
P.O. Box 120
Montreal, QC H4Z 1B7
Canada
(514) 904-9232
Web site: http://www.wada-ama.org
The WADA is an international organization that polices doping in sports.

Web Sites

Due to the changing nature of Internet links, Rosen Publishing has developed an online list of Web sites related to the subject of this book. This site is updated regularly. Please use this link to access the list:

http://www.rosenlinks.com/dis/base

FOR FURTHER READING

Egendorf, Laura K. *Performance-Enhancing Drugs*. San Diego, CA: Referencepoint Press, 2007.

Fitzhugh, Karla. *Steroids*. Chicago, IL: Heinemann Library, 2005.

Lau, Doretta. *Incredibly Disgusting Drugs: Steroids*. New York, NY: Rosen Publishing, 2008.

Levert, Susan. *The Facts About Steroids*. Tarrytown, NY: Marshall Cavendish Children's Books, 2004.

Light, Jonathan Fraser. *The Cultural Encyclopedia of Baseball*. Jefferson, NC: McFarland & Company, Inc., 2005.

Savage, Jeff. *Barry Bonds*. Minneapolis, MN: Lerner Publishing, 2008.

Shepard, Greg. *Bigger, Faster, Stronger*. Champaign, IL: Human Kinetics, 2003.

BIBLIOGRAPHY

Assael, Shaun. *Steroid Nation*. New York, NY: ESPN Books, 2007.

Bouton, Jim. *Ball Four*. New York, NY: Wiley Publishing, Inc., 1970.

Bryant, Howard. *Juicing the Game*. New York, NY: Viking, 2005.

Bryant, Howard. "Missing Link in Mitchell Report Is Attention to Records." ESPN.com, December 14, 2007. Retrieved November 5, 2008 (http://sports.espn.go.com/mlb/columns/story?id=3155244).

Canseco, José. *Juiced: Wild Times, Rampant 'Roids, Smash Hits, and How Baseball Got Big*. New York, NY: HarperCollins Publishers, Inc., 2005.

Carroll, Will, and William L. Carroll. *The Juice: The Real Story of Baseball's Drug Problems*. Chicago, IL: Ivan R. Dee, 2005.

Connolly, Dan, and Jeff Baker. "Palmeiro Learned of Failed Test in May." *Baltimore Sun*, August 3, 2005. Retrieved January 19, 2009 (http://www.

baltimoresun.com/sports/baseball/bal-te.sp.palmeiro03aug03,1,3296592. story?page=1).

Cook, Ron. "The Eighties: A Terrible Time of Trial and Error." *Pittsburgh Post-Gazette*, September 29, 2000. Retrieved November 5, 2008 (http://www. post-gazette.com/pirates/200009291980bucs3.asp).

Crasnick, Jerry. "Kicking Amphetamines." *ESPN Insider*, January 12, 2006. Retrieved November 5, 2008 (http://sports.espn.go.com/espn/ print?id=2289509&type=story).

ESPN.com. "Autopsy: Howe Had Meth in System at Time of Crash." June 28, 2006. Retrieved November 5, 2008 (http://sports.espn.go.com/mlb/news/ story?id=2503090).

ESPN.com. "The Mitchell Report: Baseball Slow to React to Players' Steroid Use." December 14, 2007. Retrieved November 5, 2008 (http://sports. espn.go.com/mlb/news/story?id=3153509).

ESPN.com. "MLB, Players' Union Agree to More Frequent Drug Testing." April 11, 2008. Retrieved November 5, 2008 (http://sports.espn.go.com/mlb/news/ story?id=3341940).

ESPN.com. "Players Listed in the Mitchell Commission Report." December 13, 2007. Retrieved November 5, 2008 (http://sports.espn.go.com/mlb/news/ story?id=3153646).

ESPN.com. "Suspensions Increasingly Unlikely for Players Named in Mitchell Report." ESPN.com, March 12, 2008. Retrieved November 5, 2008 (http:// sports.espn.go.com/mlb/spring2008/news/story?id=3290376).

ESPN.com "Tigers' Perez Tests Positive for Stimulant for Third Time." August 4, 2007. Retrieved January 24, 2009 (http://sports.espn.go.com/mlb/news/ story?id=2960193).

Fainaru-Wada, Mark, and Lance Williams. *Game of Shadows: Barry Bonds, BALCO, and the Steroids Scandal That Rocked Professional Sports*. New York, NY: Gotham Books, 2006.

Jenkins, Lee. "Popular Steroid Is at the Center of Palmeiro's Case." *New York Times*, August 3, 2005. Retrieved January 23, 2009 (http://www.nytimes.com/2005/08/03/sports/baseball/03steroids.html).

Lacayo, Rick, and Joseph N. Boyce. "The Cocaine Agonies Continue." *Time*, September 23, 1985. Retrieved November 5, 2008 (http://www.time.com/time/magazine/article/0,9171,959943,00.html).

McAlester, Keven. "Balls Out." *Dallas Observer*, June 16, 2005. Retrieved November 5, 2008 (http://www.dallasobserver.com/2005-06-16/news/balls-out).

Mitchell, George J. *Report to the Commissioner of Baseball of an Independent Investigation into the Illegal Use of Steroids and Other Performance Enhancing Substances by Players in Major League Baseball.* New York, NY: Office of the Commissioner of Baseball, 2007.

New York Times. "Mark McGwire's Pep Pills." August 27, 1998. Retrieved January 23, 2009 (http://query.nytimes.com/gst/fullpage.html?res=9801EFDD133CF934A1575BC0A96E958260).

Schoenfield, David. "Court Is in Session." ESPN.com, August 5, 2003. Retrieved November 5, 2008 (http://sports.espn.go.com/espn/page2/story?page=trials).

Shipley, Alison. "Court: Investigators Can Keep Positive Test Results." *Washington Post*, December 28, 2006. Retrieved November 5, 2008 (http://www.washingtonpost.com/wp-dyn/content/article/2006/12/27/AR2006122701142.html).

Stromberg, Gary, and Jane Merril. *The Harder They Fall: Celebrities Tell Their Real-Life Stories of Addiction and Recovery.* Center City, MN: Hazelden, 2007.

Verducci, Tom. "Steroids in Baseball: Confessions of an MVP." *Sports Illustrated*, June 3, 2002.

Wilson, Duff, and Michael Schmidt. "Missing from Mitchell Report, Sosa Is Included in Grimsley Affidavit." *New York Times*, December 21, 2007. Retrieved January 19, 2009 (http://www.nytimes.com/2007/12/21/sports/baseball/21mitchell.html?fta=y).

INDEX

A

Aaron, Hank, 13, 32
amphetamines, use of in baseball, 6–7, 9, 10, 14, 15, 21, 31
Anderson, Barry, 10–12
Anderson, Greg, 16, 19
androstenedione, 12, 14, 22

B

BALCO, 16–19, 29, 32, 38
Baseball Hall of Fame, 7, 9, 32–33, 34
Berra, Dale, 7
Bonds, Barry, 13, 15, 16, 19, 22, 32, 34
Brown, Kevin, 23

C

Caminiti, Ken, 16, 22
Canseco, José, 19, 22
Clemens, Roger, 23–25
cocaine, use of in baseball, 9, 10, 31
Conte, Victor, 19

D

drug testing, in baseball, 14–15, 20–21, 31, 38
Dykstra, Lenny, 22

E

Ellis, Dock, 10

F

fans, reaction to steroid use by players, 32, 34
Fehr, Donald, 19

G

Gagne, Eric, 22
Giambi, Jason, 15, 16–18, 19, 22
González, Juan, 22
"greenies," 6–7
Grimsley, Jason, 21–22

H

Hernandez, Keith, 9
Hill, Glenallen, 22
home run records, 12–14, 16, 32, 34
    race of 1998, 12, 35
Howe, Steve, 9
human growth hormone, use of in baseball, 4, 21, 23, 29, 31, 37, 38, 38

J

Jenkins, Ferguson, 9
Joint Drug Treatment and Prevention Program, 20, 22
Justice, David, 22–23

K

Knoblauch, Chuck, 22

M

Major League Baseball
    drug policy of, 4, 7, 12, 14–15, 20–21, 31, 37–38
    history of drug use in, 6–15
    investigation into steroid use, 19–20, 21, 22, 25

About the Author

Jason Porterfield is the author of more than twenty books for Rosen Publishing. He has written extensively on the topics of both baseball and performance-enhancing drugs, with titles including *Baseball: Rules, Tips, Strategy, and Safety*; *Baseball in the American League Central Division*; *Baseball in the National League East Division*; and *Doping: Athletes and Drugs*. He lives in Chicago.

Photo Credits

Cover (top), pp. 1, 3, 6, 16, 26, 32 © Nick Laham/Getty Images; cover (bottom) © Jed Jacobsohn/Getty Images; p. 5 © Scott Halleran/Allsport/Getty Images; p. 7 © Focus on Sport/Getty Images; p. 8 © Andrew D. Bernstein/Getty Images; pp. 10, 22, 24, 29, 34 © www.istockphoto.com; p. 11 © Pictorial Parade; pp. 13, 20, 33, 36 © AP Photos; p. 14 © Bob Rowan-Progressive Images/Corbis; p. 17 © Andy Lyons/Getty Images; p. 18 © Justin Sullivan/Getty Images; p. 23 © Scott L. Ferrell/Getty Images; p. 25 © Tim Sloan/AFP/Getty Images; p. 27 © Scott Rovak/Getty Images; p. 30 © Jim McIsaac/Getty Images; p. 35 © JamieSquire/Getty Images; p. 37 © D.E.A.

Designer: Nicole Russo; Photo Researcher: Marty Levick